Confidence Unleashed: How to Build Self-Esteem and Assertiveness

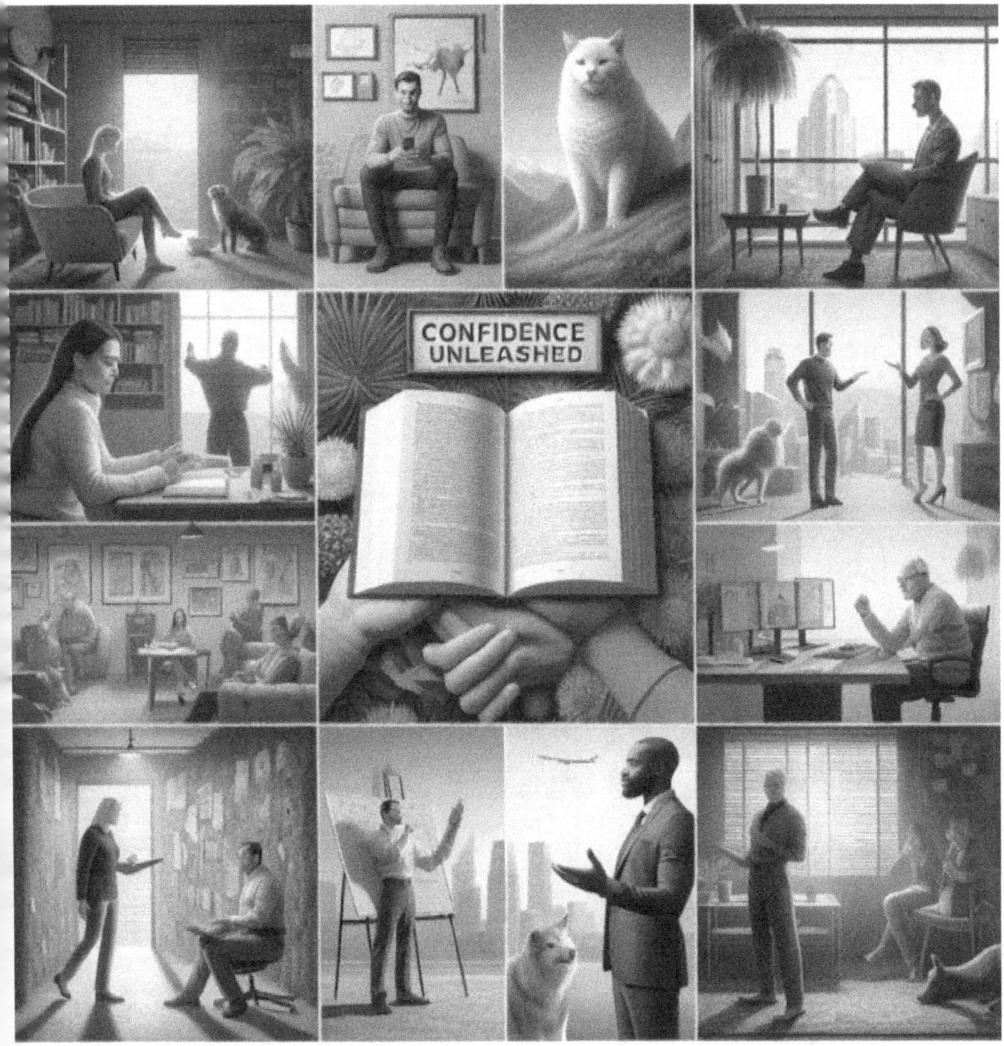

Daniel Sunoo

1. --
2. Summary
3. Chapter 2
4. Chapter 1: Understanding Self-Esteem and Assertiveness
5. Chapter 2: The Science Behind Our Thoughts and Behaviors
6. Chapter 3: Identifying Negative Patterns
7. Chapter 4: Building Blocks of Confidence
8. Chapter 5: Practical Steps to Assertiveness
9. Chapter 6: Exercises for Enhancing Self-Esteem
10. Chapter 7: Real-World Application of Assertive Communication
11. Chapter 8: Progressive Skill Building
12. Chapter 9: Overcoming Setbacks
13. Chapter 10: Long-Term Success in Confidence Maintenance
14. Chapter 11: Special Considerations in the Journey to Confidence
15. Chapter 12: Conclusion and Future Directions
16. Synopsis

Summary

Chapter 1: Understanding Self-Esteem and Assertiveness 3
1.1 The Psychological Foundations of Confidence 3
1.2 Defining Self-Esteem and Assertiveness 5
1.3 Impact of Low Self-Esteem on Personal and Professional Life 7
Chapter 2: The Science Behind Our Thoughts and Behaviors 9
2.1 Insights from Cognitive Behavioral Therapy (CBT) 9
2.2 Contributions of Social Psychology 1:
2.3 Neuroscience Perspectives on Behavior and Thought Processes 1:
Chapter 3: Identifying Negative Patterns 1:
3.1 Recognizing Self-Sabotaging Thoughts 1:
3.2 Analyzing Behavioral Patterns That Undermine Confidence 1'
3.3 Strategies to Break the Cycle of Negativity 1!
Chapter 4: Building Blocks of Confidence 2
4.1 Establishing a Positive Mindset 2
4.2 Role of Self-Awareness in Personal Growth 2:
4.3 Embracing Vulnerability as Strength 2<
Chapter 5: Practical Steps to Assertiveness 2(
5.1 Developing Clear Communication Skills 2(
5.2 Setting Healthy Boundaries 2:
5.3 Techniques for Effective Conflict Resolution 3(
Chapter 6: Exercises for Enhancing Self-Esteem 3:
6.1 Daily Affirmations and Their Power 3:
6.2 Visualization Techniques for Confidence 3<
6.3 Journaling for Emotional Clarity 3(

Chapter 7: Real-World Application of Assertive Communication
7.1 Handling Criticism Constructively
7.2 Assertiveness in Workplace Interactions
7.3 Navigating Social Situations with Confidence
Chapter 8: Progressive Skill Building
8.1 Incremental Learning Approach to Skill Enhancement
8.2 Role-Playing Scenarios to Practice Responses
8.3 Feedback Mechanisms for Continuous Improvement
Chapter 9: Overcoming Setbacks
9.1 Identifying Triggers and Learning from Failures
9.2 Maintaining Motivation During Challenges
9.3 Adaptive Strategies for Resilience
Chapter 10: Long-Term Success in Confidence Maintenance
10.1 Incorporating Mindfulness into Daily Routine
10.2 Continuous Learning and Adaptation
10.3 Building a Support Network
Chapter 11: Special Considerations in the Journey to Confidence
11.1 Addressing Anxiety and Depression
11.2 Tailoring Approaches for Different Personality Types
11.3 Cultural Influences on Assertiveness
Chapter 12: Conclusion and Future Directions
12.1 Summarizing Key Takeaways
12.2 Encouraging Lifelong Practice
12.3 Resources for Further Exploration

Understanding Self-Esteem and Assertiveness

1.1 The Psychological Foundations of Confidence

The journey to understanding self-esteem and assertiveness begins with a deep dive into the psychological foundations of confidence. This exploration is crucial as it lays the groundwork for all subsequent strategies aimed at enhancing personal empowerment and assertive communication. Confidence, fundamentally rooted in our psychological makeup, is influenced by a variety of cognitive, emotional, and behavioral factors that shape how we perceive ourselves and interact with the world.

At its core, confidence stems from beliefs about our abilities and value as individuals. Cognitive theories suggest that these beliefs are formed through experiences and interactions from early childhood onwards. Positive reinforcements and successes contribute to a robust sense of self-efficacy, while negative experiences and failures may lead to doubts about one's capabilities and worth. Cognitive Behavioral Therapy (CBT) provides insights into how these thought patterns can be identified and reshaped to foster a more positive self-view, thereby enhancing confidence.

Emotionally, confidence is closely linked to feelings of security and self-acceptance. Research in neuroscience has shown that emotional responses are governed by complex brain networks that can be trained over time through mindfulness practices and emotional intelligence development. By learning to manage emotions effectively, individuals can maintain a steadier level of confidence even in challenging situations.

Behaviorally, confident individuals exhibit assertiveness that allows them to express themselves freely and stand up for their beliefs without infringing on the rights of others. Social psychology highlights the role of social interactions in developing assertive behavior patterns. Engaging positively with others can reinforce self-assured behaviors and encourage more frequent displays of confidence.

In conclusion, understanding the psychological foundations of confidence involves examining how thoughts, emotions, and behaviors are interconnected in shaping our self-esteem levels. By addressing each aspect with targeted strategies such as CBT for cognitive restructuring, emotional intelligence training for managing feelings, and social skills development for behavioral adjustments, individuals can lay a solid foundation for building lasting confidence.

1.2 Defining Self-Esteem and Assertiveness

Self-esteem is an internal measure of how much we value ourselves, which significantly influences our life choices and interactions. It encompasses beliefs about one's own worth and capabilities, as well as emotional states such as triumph, despair, pride, and shame. Psychologists often describe self-esteem as a lasting sense of self-compiled from beliefs formed by experiences and interpreted through individual frameworks of thought.

Assertiveness, on the other hand, is a behavioral skill that refers to an individual's ability to express their thoughts, feelings, and needs in a direct, honest, and appropriate way. It involves respecting oneself and others when communicating. This trait is not about being aggressive or passive; rather, it's about being forthright about your desires without violating the rights of others. Assertiveness can be seen as a practical application of one's self-esteem in interpersonal situations.

The relationship between self-esteem and assertiveness is deeply intertwined. High self-esteem often empowers individuals to act assertively because they feel confident in their intrinsic value and believe their needs are important. Conversely, practicing assertiveness can strengthen self-esteem by reinforcing the individual's belief in their own competence and worthiness.

Developing both high self-esteem and effective assertiveness skills requires introspection and practice. For instance, cognitive-behavioral approaches can help individuals recognize negative thought patterns that undermine self-esteem or inhibit assertive behavior. Techniques such as role-playing or assertive communication training can also provide practical experience in expressing oneself confidently.

Moreover, societal influences play a crucial role in shaping these traits. Cultural norms dictate acceptable levels of assertiveness and influence how individuals perceive their own value. Understanding these external factors can help individuals navigate between maintaining personal integrity while adapting to social expectations.

In conclusion, defining self-esteem involves recognizing it as an internal state influenced by personal judgments of worthiness while understanding assertiveness as the external expression of this esteem through communication with others. Both are essential for psychological health and successful social interactions.

1.3 Impact of Low Self-Esteem on Personal and Professional Life

The repercussions of low self-esteem extend deeply into both personal and professional spheres, often creating a cycle of negative experiences that can hinder an individual's overall quality of life. In personal relationships, low self-esteem can lead to a pattern of dysfunctional interactions. Individuals may struggle with feelings of unworthiness, which can result in either excessive clinginess or withdrawal from relationships due to fear of rejection or criticism. This lack of confidence can make it difficult for them to assert their needs or set healthy boundaries, potentially leading to unbalanced relationships where their desires and needs are consistently sidelined.

In the professional context, low self-esteem can be equally debilitating. It often manifests as poor job performance due to a fear of taking on challenging tasks or asserting one's ideas in collaborative settings. Employees with low self-esteem might avoid seeking promotions or additional responsibilities because they doubt their capabilities or fear failure, thereby stunting their career growth. Moreover, such individuals might overly criticize themselves for minor mistakes, further diminishing their confidence and contributing to a persistent sense of inadequacy at work.

The impact on decision-making processes is another significant consequence of low self-esteem in both personal and professional life. Individuals may exhibit indecisiveness, constantly second-guessing themselves or deferring decisions to others out of a lack of trust in their own judgment. This can lead to missed opportunities and potential regret, reinforcing feelings of incompetence and failure.

Furthermore, the stress associated with low self-esteem can contribute to physical and mental health issues. Chronic stress may lead to conditions such as anxiety, depression, or even physical ailments like hypertension or digestive problems caused by constant tension and worry about one's self-worth and abilities.

Addressing these challenges requires a multifaceted approach that includes therapy, support groups, personal development activities, and possibly changes in environment or job roles where one feels more valued and empowered. Enhancing self-esteem is not just about changing how one feels about oneself but also about creating external conditions that reinforce positive self-perception and functional interpersonal dynamics.

The Science Behind Our Thoughts and Behavi

2.1 Insights from Cognitive Behavioral Therapy (CBT)

Cognitive Behavioral Therapy (CBT) is a highly effective psychological treatment that has revolutionized the understanding and management of self-esteem and assertiveness issues. Rooted in both cognitive and behavioral psychology, CBT operates on the fundamental premise that our thoughts, feelings, and behaviors are interconnected, and that altering one can substantially change the others. This therapy provides practical tools for individuals to reshape their thought patterns to foster better self-esteem and more assertive behavior.

At its core, CBT involves identifying negative or false beliefs and testing or restructuring them into more positive, realistic thoughts. This process begins with awareness, as individuals learn to recognize their automatic thoughts—the immediate, often subconscious, thoughts that pop up in response to specific stimuli. These thoughts can be deeply ingrained and skewed towards negativity or pessimism, particularly in individuals with low self-esteem or those who struggle with assertiveness.

CBT techniques encourage a detailed examination of these automatic thoughts by questioning their validity and exploring alternative viewpoints. For instance, someone who believes "I am not good enough to voice my opinion" is guided to explore this belief's origin, challenge its accuracy, and consider past instances where they successfully expressed their thoughts. Through exercises like journaling or role-playing, CBT helps individuals practice new ways of thinking and behaving that promote confidence and assertiveness.

The behavioral component of CBT also plays a crucial role in building self-esteem and assertiveness. Behavioral experiments are used to test the beliefs against reality through controlled exposure to feared situations. For example, someone afraid of public speaking might start by speaking in front of a mirror, progress to speaking in front of a small group of friends, and eventually address larger groups as confidence grows.

Moreover, CBT emphasizes the development of personal coping strategies that enhance resilience against setbacks in self-esteem or moments of non-assertiveness. Techniques such as mindfulness meditation strengthen an individual's ability to remain present-focused during stressful situations rather than succumbing to overwhelming negative emotions or destructive thought patterns.

In summary, Cognitive Behavioral Therapy offers powerful insights into how changing one's thought patterns can lead directly to improved self-confidence and enhanced interpersonal effectiveness through assertiveness training. By systematically breaking down fears associated with self-expression and replacing them with empowering beliefs, CBT equips individuals with the skills necessary for personal empowerment in various aspects of life.

2.2 Contributions of Social Psychology

Social psychology, a vibrant subfield of psychology, explores how individual thoughts, feelings, and behaviors are influenced by the social context. This field has made significant contributions to understanding human behavior in social settings, emphasizing the powerful role of social influence on personal and group actions.

One of the key areas where social psychology has been particularly influential is in the study of attitudes and attitude change. Researchers have developed theories such as the Theory of Planned Behavior and Cognitive Dissonance Theory to explain how attitudes form and how they can be changed. These theories help in understanding everything from consumer behavior to political campaigning, illustrating how subtle changes in communication can significantly alter people's responses.

Social psychologists have also deeply explored the concept of social conformity and obedience. Classic experiments by Asch on conformity and Milgram on obedience highlight how strong the pressure to conform can be, even against one's own judgment or moral compass. These studies have profound implications for educational practices, workplace environments, and legal systems by showing how societal norms powerfully dictate individual behavior.

Another significant contribution is the understanding of group dynamics. Social psychologists examine how individuals behave differently in groups compared to when they are alone. Concepts such as group polarization, where discussions within a group lead members to adopt more extreme positions, and social facilitation, which looks at how performance changes when others are watching, are central to this study. These insights are crucial for improving team performance in organizations and understanding phenomena like public riots or collective problem-solving.

Furthermore, social psychology contributes extensively to conflict resolution and intergroup relations. The Contact Hypothesis suggests that under appropriate conditions interpersonal contact is one of the most effective ways to reduce prejudice between majority and minority group members. This hypothesis has informed numerous programs worldwide that aim to reduce ethnic and racial conflicts by promoting interaction between diverse groups.

In summary, social psychology offers invaluable insights into human behavior by focusing on the influence of interpersonal relationships and societal structures. Its findings not only enrich our theoretical knowledge but also apply practically across various sectors including marketing, policy-making, education, and beyond.

2.3 Neuroscience Perspectives on Behavior and Thought Processes

The field of neuroscience has significantly advanced our understanding of how biological processes underpin behaviors and thought processes. By examining the neural mechanisms that orchestrate our cognitive functions and behaviors, neuroscientists provide insights into the complex interplay between the brain's structure and its functionalities.

One critical area of focus within neuroscience is the study of neural circuits and how they influence behavior. These circuits are networks of neurons that communicate through synapses, transmitting signals that affect everything from reflexive responses to complex decision-making. Techniques such as functional magnetic resonance imaging (fMRI) and positron emission tomography (PET) scans allow researchers to observe these circuits in action, linking specific patterns of brain activity with particular behavioral outcomes.

Neuroplasticity is another significant concept in this domain, referring to the brain's ability to reorganize itself by forming new neural connections throughout life. This adaptability is crucial for learning new skills, recovering from brain injuries, and adapting to new environments or changes in one's life. Studies on neuroplasticity have shown how experiences reshape the neural pathways, fundamentally altering how we think, learn, and behave.

The role of neurotransmitters in regulating mood and behavior also underscores a vital aspect of neuroscience. These chemical messengers facilitate communication between neurons across synapses. Imbalances or disruptions in neurotransmitter systems can lead to psychological disorders such as depression, schizophrenia, and anxiety. Understanding these systems thus not only aids in comprehending normal brain function but also highlights targets for therapeutic interventions in mental health disorders.

Finally, the integration of genetics with neuroscience has opened new avenues for exploring how inherited traits may predispose individuals to certain behaviors or thought patterns. Through genome-wide association studies (GWAS), scientists identify genetic variations correlated with risks for developing psychiatric conditions like bipolar disorder or ADHD. This genetic perspective supports a more personalized approach to treatment strategies that cater specifically to an individual's unique genetic makeup.

In conclusion, neuroscience provides a profound depth of insight into human behavior by elucidating the biological foundations of our thoughts and actions. From studying neural circuits to exploring genetic influences on behavior, this field continues to unravel the complexities behind what makes us who we are.

3 Identifying Negative Patterns

3.1 Recognizing Self-Sabotaging Thoughts

Understanding and addressing self-sabotaging thoughts is crucial for personal growth and effective communication. These are the internal dialogues that often lead to decreased confidence and hinder our ability to assert ourselves in various situations. Recognizing these patterns is the first step towards developing a healthier, more assertive communication style.

Self-sabotaging thoughts typically manifest as negative inner critiques that challenge one's own abilities or worth. Common examples include thoughts like "I'm not good enough," "I can't do this," or "No one cares about what I have to say." These thoughts can stem from past experiences, societal influences, or even the fear of failure. They not only erode self-esteem but also prevent individuals from taking actions that align with their true potential.

To combat these destructive thought patterns, it is essential to first become aware of them. This involves mindful observation of one's own thoughts and feelings without judgment. By acknowledging these thoughts when they arise and understanding their origin, individuals can begin to question their validity and reshape their thinking patterns.

Identify triggers: Recognize situations or emotions that typically elicit self-sabotaging thoughts.

Challenge negativity: Confront these negative thoughts with evidence that contradicts them, reinforcing a more positive and realistic perspective.

Rewrite the narrative: Replace self-sabotaging thoughts with affirmations or positive statements that reflect one's abilities and worth.

Incorporating techniques from cognitive behavioral therapy (CBT) can be particularly effective in this process. CBT encourages individuals to break down overwhelming problems into smaller parts, making it easier to change negative thought patterns into more positive ones gradually. Additionally, engaging in regular reflective practices such as journaling or speaking with a therapist can provide deeper insights into why these self-sabotaging thoughts occur and how to effectively address them.

Ultimately, recognizing and overcoming self-sabotaging thoughts is a journey towards self-empowerment. It allows individuals not only to build greater resilience but also enhances their ability to communicate assertively in both personal and professional settings. By continuously practicing these strategies, one can maintain a healthy level of self-esteem and develop lasting confidence.

3.2 Analyzing Behavioral Patterns That Undermine Confidence

Building on the understanding of self-sabotaging thoughts, it is equally important to recognize and analyze behavioral patterns that undermine confidence. These behaviors often manifest subtly but have significant impacts on personal and professional growth.

One common behavior is the avoidance of challenges. When individuals consistently shy away from tasks or situations that seem difficult, they inadvertently reinforce the belief that they are not capable enough to handle them. This avoidance can become a habitual response that limits opportunities for success and personal development.

Another detrimental pattern is over-apologizing. Frequent apologies, especially when unwarranted, can diminish one's perceived competence and authority. It sends a message of self-doubt and uncertainty, reducing the individual's credibility in the eyes of others.

Perfectionism is also a behavior that undermines confidence. While striving for excellence is positive, setting unrealistically high standards can lead to excessive self-criticism and procrastination. Perfectionists often hesitate to start or complete tasks unless they feel certain of flawless execution, which can stall progress and foster feelings of inadequacy.

Social withdrawal is another behavior linked to low confidence. Individuals may isolate themselves due to fear of judgment or rejection, missing out on valuable interactions that could build their social skills and self-assurance.

To counter these behaviors, it is crucial to first acknowledge their presence without self-judgment. Reflective practices such as journaling or discussions with a therapist can help in identifying specific instances where these behaviors emerge. Setting small, manageable goals can gradually build confidence in handling challenging situations without resorting to avoidance or over-apologizing.

Engaging in assertiveness training programs can also be beneficial. These programs teach how to express oneself confidently and clearly, balancing one's own needs with those of others. Additionally, mindfulness techniques can aid in managing perfectionist tendencies by fostering an acceptance of 'good enough' and reducing the fear of making mistakes.

In conclusion, recognizing and modifying these undermining behavioral patterns plays a critical role in boosting confidence. By actively addressing these behaviors through strategic interventions and consistent practice, individuals can enhance their ability to navigate various aspects of life with greater assurance and effectiveness.

3.3 Strategies to Break the Cycle of Negativity

Breaking free from negative behavioral patterns is essential for personal growth and confidence. This section explores effective strategies that can help individuals overcome these self-sabotaging habits.

The first step in breaking the cycle of negativity is cultivating self-awareness. Recognizing when and why negative behaviors occur can be transformative. For instance, maintaining a reflective journal where one records thoughts and feelings surrounding specific incidents can illuminate patterns of negativity such as avoidance or over-apologizing.

Another powerful strategy involves redefining one's mindset through cognitive restructuring. This psychological technique challenges and changes unhelpful thoughts and beliefs. By questioning the validity of negative thoughts and replacing them with more positive, realistic ones, individuals can reduce instances of perfectionism and social withdrawal.

Setting achievable goals is also crucial in combating negative behaviors. Small, manageable objectives encourage taking steps forward rather than shying away from challenges due to fear of failure or judgment. Success in these smaller goals builds momentum and confidence, gradually diminishing the power of negative patterns.

Engagement in mindfulness practices offers another beneficial approach. Techniques such as meditation, deep breathing exercises, or yoga help individuals stay present and focused, reducing the impact of stressors that often trigger negative behaviors like social withdrawal or perfectionism.

Social support plays a pivotal role in overcoming negativity as well. Sharing experiences with friends, family, or support groups can provide encouragement and accountability. Additionally, professional help from therapists or counselors can offer guidance tailored to individual needs, helping to navigate through complex emotional landscapes.

Finally, embracing self-compassion is essential when working through negative patterns. Instead of harsh self-criticism during setbacks, treating oneself with kindness and understanding fosters resilience against future negativity.

In conclusion, breaking the cycle of negativity involves a multifaceted approach including self-awareness, cognitive restructuring, goal setting, mindfulness practices, social support, and self-compassion. Implementing these strategies not only diminishes detrimental behaviors but also enhances overall mental health and well-being.

4 Building Blocks of Confidence

4.1 Establishing a Positive Mindset

Establishing a positive mindset is the cornerstone of building confidence and self-esteem. This section explores how cultivating such a mindset can significantly influence one's ability to assert themselves in various aspects of life. A positive mindset not only enhances self-perception but also improves interactions with others, leading to more successful and fulfilling relationships.

The first step in fostering a positive mindset is understanding the impact of cognitive biases on our thoughts. Cognitive distortions such as 'filtering' (focusing on negative details) or 'catastrophizing' (anticipating the worst) can severely dampen one's confidence. Awareness and identification of these patterns are crucial as they form the basis for cognitive restructuring, a technique used in cognitive behavioral therapy (CBT). By challenging these negative thoughts and replacing them with more balanced and constructive ones, individuals can begin to see improvements in their mental outlook.

Another vital aspect is the role of gratitude in mental health. Regularly practicing gratitude can shift attention away from toxic emotions and towards appreciating what one has. This shift not only increases positivity but also enhances overall well-being by reducing stress and anxiety. Techniques such as maintaining a gratitude journal or meditating on things one is thankful for each day can be beneficial practices to integrate into daily routines.

Moreover, visualization techniques serve as powerful tools for establishing a positive mindset. Envisioning successful outcomes and engaging with this success emotionally prepares one mentally for real-life challenges, enhancing self-assurance when facing similar situations. This method not only boosts confidence but also conditions the brain to react positively to challenges, viewing them as opportunities rather than obstacles.

In conclusion, developing a positive mindset involves recognizing and adjusting cognitive distortions, practicing gratitude, and employing visualization techniques. These strategies collectively contribute to building a robust foundation for sustained personal growth and confidence. Embracing these practices enables individuals to transform their approach to life's challenges, fostering resilience and assertiveness that propel them towards achieving their goals.

4.2 Role of Self-Awareness in Personal Growth

Self-awareness is a pivotal element in the journey of personal growth and development. It involves a deep understanding of one's thoughts, emotions, strengths, weaknesses, and behaviors. By cultivating self-awareness, individuals can make more informed decisions, improve their relationships, and navigate life's challenges with greater competence and resilience.

The process of becoming self-aware begins with introspection. This reflective practice allows individuals to examine their internal states and preferences without judgment. Introspection can be facilitated through various methods such as journaling, meditation, or therapy. These activities help to uncover underlying motivations and desires that influence behavior and decision-making.

Another critical aspect of self-awareness is emotional intelligence. Understanding and managing one's emotions is crucial for maintaining personal well-being and fostering strong interpersonal relationships.

Emotional intelligence includes skills such as emotional regulation, empathy, motivation, and social skills—all of which are enhanced by a heightened sense of self-awareness.

Feedback from others also plays an essential role in developing self-awareness. Constructive criticism helps individuals recognize patterns they may not see themselves. Engaging in honest conversations with friends, family members, or colleagues provides external perspectives that can challenge one's self-perception and lead to significant insights.

Moreover, setting personal boundaries is an important outcome of self-awareness that contributes to personal growth. When individuals understand their limits and needs clearly, they are better equipped to communicate these boundaries to others. This not only enhances one's respect for oneself but also teaches others how to interact with them appropriately.

In conclusion, the role of self-awareness in personal growth cannot be overstated. It serves as the foundation upon which many other personal development skills are built. By fostering a deeper understanding of oneself through introspection, emotional intelligence training, receptive feedback mechanisms, and clear boundary setting practices—individuals empower themselves to lead more fulfilling lives both personally and professionally.

4.3 Embracing Vulnerability as Strength

In the journey of personal development, embracing vulnerability emerges as a profound strength, contrary to traditional perceptions of it as a weakness. This section explores how vulnerability can catalyze growth, foster deeper connections, and enhance resilience.

Vulnerability involves exposing oneself to the possibility of emotional exposure, risks, and uncertainty. It is a courageous act of opening up one's true self to others, which can lead to significant personal transformation. By embracing vulnerability, individuals allow themselves to experience genuine emotions and interactions, which are essential for building trust and strengthening relationships.

One of the key benefits of being vulnerable is the enhancement of empathy both from oneself towards others and vice versa. When people share their fears, failures, or uncertainties openly, they become more relatable and approachable. This mutual understanding can bridge gaps between individuals, fostering a supportive environment that encourages sharing and collaboration.

Moreover, vulnerability acts as a catalyst for innovation and creativity. The willingness to fail and learn from mistakes is crucial in any creative process. In environments where vulnerability is embraced, individuals feel safe to express novel ideas and experiment without the fear of judgment or failure. This openness not only leads to personal growth but also drives collective advancement within teams and organizations.

However, embracing vulnerability requires mindful practice and often begins with self-awareness—understanding one's emotions and triggers. Techniques such as reflective journaling or mindfulness meditation can help individuals become more attuned to their feelings and comfortable with expressing them openly.

In conclusion, while vulnerability might seem daunting initially due to societal stigmas associated with showing weakness or uncertainty, its acceptance can profoundly impact personal development. It allows for authentic experiences that are crucial for meaningful relationships and effective communication. By fostering an environment where vulnerability is viewed as a strength rather than a weakness, individuals empower themselves and those around them to lead richer, more fulfilling lives.

5 Practical Steps to Assertiveness

5.1 Developing Clear Communication Skills

Effective communication is the cornerstone of assertiveness, enabling individuals to express their thoughts and feelings clearly and confidently. This section explores the essential techniques for developing clear communication skills, which are vital for enhancing self-esteem and assertiveness as discussed in "Confidence Unleashed."

To begin with, clarity in communication involves both the articulation of words and the organization of thoughts. It is crucial to be concise and specific to avoid misunderstandings. This can be achieved by planning what you want to say ahead of time and practicing your delivery. Techniques such as 'think before you speak' and 'structuring your thoughts' can significantly improve the quality of interactions.

Active listening plays a pivotal role in clear communication. It involves fully concentrating on the speaker, understanding their message, responding thoughtfully, and remembering the discussion. This skill ensures mutual understanding and builds trust between parties, facilitating more effective exchanges of ideas.

Use simple language that can be easily understood rather than complex vocabulary that might confuse listeners.

Maintain eye contact to show engagement and sincerity.

Utilize body language effectively—gestures like nodding show attentiveness while maintaining an open stance indicates receptiveness.

An often overlooked aspect of clear communication is the ability to ask questions. Questions not only clarify what the other person has said but also demonstrate interest in their thoughts or feelings. Moreover, paraphrasing or summarizing what others have said can reassure them that they are being heard correctly.

Feedback is another critical element in developing clear communication skills. Providing constructive feedback helps others understand where they stand and encourages personal growth. Similarly, receiving feedback openly allows for self-improvement and fosters a culture of continuous learning within relationships or teams.

In conclusion, mastering clear communication requires practice and mindfulness about how one's messages are delivered and received. By focusing on these areas—articulation, active listening, body language, questioning, summarizing, and feedback—individuals can enhance their assertive capabilities significantly. These skills not only contribute to personal development but also improve interpersonal relationships both professionally and personally.

5.2 Setting Healthy Boundaries

Setting healthy boundaries is a fundamental aspect of developing assertiveness and maintaining personal well-being. It involves understanding and articulating one's limits in various aspects of life, including emotional, physical, and mental domains. Establishing these boundaries helps individuals protect their self-esteem, conserve emotional energy, and engage in mutually respectful relationships.

Boundaries can be thought of as guidelines or rules that a person creates to identify reasonable, safe, and permissible ways for others to behave towards them. These also determine how they will respond when someone steps outside those limits. The process of setting these boundaries starts with self-reflection; recognizing what you are comfortable with and what you value most.

Communicating your boundaries clearly is crucial. This should be done assertively but respectfully, ensuring that your tone and choice of words convey your needs without aggression or passivity. For instance, if someone asks too much of your time, you might say: "I value our relationship, but I need to ensure I have enough time for other responsibilities. Let's find a suitable time that works for both of us."

It is also essential to enforce the boundaries once they are set. If someone repeatedly ignores your boundaries, you need to address the behavior immediately. This might involve reiterating your boundary more firmly or limiting contact with the person who fails to respect your limits.

An often overlooked aspect of setting healthy boundaries is respecting others' limits as well. By understanding and honoring the boundaries set by others, mutual respect is maintained which fosters healthier interactions.

In conclusion, setting healthy boundaries is not about isolation or unnecessary rigidity but about fostering empowerment and respect within interpersonal relationships. It requires continuous practice and dedication to maintain these limits effectively in various situations.

Identify personal values and limits through introspection.

Communicate boundaries clearly using assertive communication techniques.

Maintain consistency in enforcing these boundaries.

Show respect for others' boundaries as part of reciprocal interaction.

This approach not only enhances individual well-being but also improves the quality of interactions in both personal and professional contexts.

5.3 Techniques for Effective Conflict Resolution

Effective conflict resolution is crucial in maintaining healthy interpersonal relationships and fostering a positive environment, whether in personal or professional settings. This section explores various techniques that can be employed to resolve conflicts constructively.

The first step in effective conflict resolution is active listening. It involves fully concentrating on the speaker, understanding their message, providing feedback, and deferring judgment. Active listening helps clarify misunderstandings and shows respect for the speaker's opinions, which can de-escalate tensions.

Another vital technique is the use of "I" statements. When conflicts arise, emotions can run high, and it might be tempting to blame or accuse others which only fuels the conflict. "I" statements allow individuals to express their feelings and thoughts without blaming the other party. For example, saying "I feel frustrated when meetings start late" rather than "You are always late to meetings" can prevent the other person from becoming defensive.

Emphasizing common goals is also essential in resolving conflicts. By reminding all parties involved of the overarching objectives they share, it becomes easier to move from opposing positions towards a unified solution. This approach shifts the focus from individual desires to collective aims.

Negotiation skills are equally important; they involve give-and-take where both parties make concessions to reach a mutually acceptable solution. Effective negotiation requires clear communication, understanding of both sides' needs, and creative problem-solving to find a compromise that satisfies everyone involved.

Finally, seeking mediation can be an effective approach when internal resolution efforts fail. A neutral third party can facilitate dialogue between conflicting parties to help them find a solution that is agreeable to all involved.

In conclusion, mastering these techniques requires patience, practice, and dedication but leads to more harmonious interactions and strengthens relationships by addressing conflicts constructively rather than allowing them to fester.

Practice active listening to ensure all parties feel heard.

Use "I" statements to express personal feelings without casting blame.

Focus on common goals to align conflicting parties towards a unified objective.

Hone negotiation skills for effective give-and-take discussions.

Consider mediation as an option when direct resolution methods do not succeed.

This comprehensive approach not only resolves disputes but also promotes a culture of respect and cooperation among individuals or groups involved.

6 Exercises for Enhancing Self-Esteem

6.1 Daily Affirmations and Their Power

Daily affirmations are simple, positive statements declaring specific goals in their completed states. Despite their simplicity, these powerful utterances can shift your mindset, boost your self-confidence, and strengthen your decision-making skills. The practice of repeating affirmations daily helps to reprogram the subconscious mind, encouraging us to believe in the potential of our actions and to maintain a positive perspective regardless of any setbacks or challenges.

Affirmations harness the brain's neuroplasticity, its ability to form and reorganize synaptic connections, especially in response to learning or experience. When we verbally affirm our dreams and ambitions, we are instantly empowered with a deep sense of reassurance that our wishful words will become reality. This psychological reinforcement boosts our sense of self-worth and can significantly alter the neural pathways responsible for negative thoughts and toxic behaviors.

The effectiveness of daily affirmations has been supported by various scientific studies which suggest that consistent affirmation practice can decrease stress, increase feelings of self-worth, and improve performance under pressure. For instance, a study published in the journal *Psychological Science* revealed that participants who practiced self-affirmations were more likely to perform better on tasks they were initially anxious about compared to those who did not.

In conclusion, while daily affirmations may seem like just words at first glance, their real power lies in their ability to remind us of our strengths and goals. By integrating affirmative practices into everyday life, individuals can foster enduring changes in their mental outlooks and overall emotional health.

Creating Effective Affirmations: For affirmations to be effective, they must be present tense, positive, personal and specific. For example, instead of saying "I will be successful," a more effective affirmation would be "I am successful in achieving my goals."

Consistency is Key: Regular repetition increases the efficacy of affirmations because it gradually changes the way you think and feel about yourself. Morning routines are particularly potent times for affirmations as they set a positive tone for the day.

Cultivating an Affirmative Environment: Surrounding yourself with people who uplift you can enhance the impact of your affirmations. Positive social interactions can reinforce the messages you are telling yourself.

6.2 Visualization Techniques for Confidence

Visualization techniques are a powerful tool for building confidence and self-esteem, complementing the affirmations discussed in the previous section. By creating vivid, positive mental images of success, individuals can condition their minds to anticipate and manifest these outcomes in real life. This process not only enhances self-belief but also prepares one mentally to face challenges and seize opportunities.

The effectiveness of visualization lies in its ability to engage the brain's regions associated with actual performance. According to neuroscience research, imagining yourself performing a task activates many of the same neural networks that are involved when physically performing the task. This mental rehearsal primes the body and mind, reducing anxiety and improving overall performance when the actual situation occurs.

To begin with visualization, find a quiet space where you can relax without interruptions. Close your eyes and take deep breaths to achieve a state of calmness. Start envisioning a specific goal or scenario in which you wish to be confident. Picture it as vividly as possible: imagine what you see, hear, feel, and even smell if relevant. For instance, if your goal is to deliver a successful presentation, visualize yourself speaking clearly and confidently, the audience reacting positively, and you feeling satisfied with your performance.

It is crucial that these visualizations are imbued with positive emotions; feel the joy of achieving your goal or the pride in overcoming a challenge. These emotions will reinforce your belief in your ability to succeed. Additionally, regularly practicing visualization can help solidify these images and sensations in your memory, making it easier to recall them when needed.

For those new to this practice, it might initially be challenging to maintain focus or create detailed images. However, like any skill, visualization becomes easier and more effective with regular practice. Some people might find it helpful to listen to guided imagery recordings or use apps designed specifically for visualization exercises.

In conclusion, integrating visualization techniques into daily routines can significantly boost one's confidence levels. By mentally simulating successful outcomes regularly, individuals not only enhance their mental preparedness but also foster a resilient mindset capable of tackling various life situations confidently.

6.3 Journaling for Emotional Clarity

Journaling is a potent tool for enhancing emotional clarity and self-awareness, serving as a reflective practice that allows individuals to articulate and process their feelings. By regularly writing down thoughts and emotions, people can gain insights into their behavioral patterns and emotional triggers, which is crucial for personal growth and improving self-esteem.

The act of journaling helps in detangling complex emotions and laying them out clearly on paper. This process not only aids in understanding one's emotional responses but also contributes to stress reduction. When individuals write about their experiences, they often find that they can release the intensity of these emotions, leading to a sense of calmness and control.

To begin journaling for emotional clarity, it is helpful to maintain a daily routine where you dedicate time to reflect on the day's events and your feelings about them. Start by describing the events that had the most emotional impact on your day. Note any strong reactions or feelings you experienced. As you write, try not to judge your feelings but rather allow yourself to feel them fully.

Another effective technique within journaling is the exploration of recurring themes or patterns. Over time, as you review past entries, you might notice specific situations or interactions that consistently trigger negative emotions such as anxiety or anger. Recognizing these patterns is the first step towards managing them more effectively.

Moreover, journaling can be therapeutic in managing mental health issues such as depression or anxiety. It provides a safe outlet for expressing difficult emotions without fear of judgment or repercussion. For those who struggle with expressing themselves verbally, writing down thoughts can be an easier alternative to vocal communication.

In conclusion, integrating journaling into your daily life can significantly enhance your emotional clarity and self-understanding. This practice not only helps in recognizing and regulating emotions but also supports overall mental health and resilience. Regularly engaging with this tool empowers individuals to take charge of their emotional well-being and fosters a deeper connection with oneself.

Real-World Application of Assertive Communication

7.1 Handling Criticism Constructively

In the journey toward self-improvement and assertive communication, one of the most challenging yet vital skills to master is handling criticism constructively. This section delves into practical strategies that empower individuals to transform potentially negative experiences into opportunities for personal growth and enhanced communication.

Criticism, whether constructive or destructive, can trigger emotional responses that may cloud judgment and lead to defensive reactions. The first step in dealing with criticism effectively is to develop a mindset that views feedback as a valuable tool for learning rather than a personal attack. This shift in perspective requires a deep understanding of one's own emotions and triggers, which can be cultivated through mindfulness practices and reflective exercises.

Once an individual adopts a receptive attitude towards criticism, the next step involves actively listening to the feedback without interrupting or jumping to conclusions. Active listening not only shows respect for the critic but also provides a clearer understanding of the points being made. It's important during this stage to ask clarifying questions if certain aspects of the criticism are unclear or seem unfounded.

After fully processing the received criticism, it is crucial to evaluate its validity objectively. This involves separating factual content from emotional tone and considering how the feedback aligns with personal or professional goals. If the critique is valid, developing an actionable plan for addressing the issues highlighted can help turn criticism into a constructive force that fosters improvement and learning.

To reinforce these skills, it is beneficial to engage in role-playing exercises where individuals can practice receiving and responding to various forms of feedback. These simulations help build confidence and fluency in using assertive communication techniques in real-world scenarios.

However, not all criticism will be useful or delivered in good faith. In such cases, assertiveness becomes key: responding politely yet firmly by setting boundaries on acceptable communication styles or pointing out misunderstandings can prevent future occurrences of unconstructive criticism while maintaining one's dignity and self-respect.

In conclusion, handling criticism constructively is not just about managing external feedback but also about internal growth and resilience. By embracing criticism as an opportunity for development and employing assertive communication strategies, individuals can enhance their interpersonal relationships and advance their personal and professional objectives.

7.2 Assertiveness in Workplace Interactions

Assertiveness in workplace interactions is essential for maintaining a healthy, productive work environment. This skill enables individuals to communicate their ideas, needs, and concerns effectively without infringing on the rights of others. It plays a crucial role in managing conflicts, negotiating compromises, and fostering mutual respect among colleagues.

One of the primary benefits of assertive communication at work is its impact on professional relationships. By expressing oneself clearly and respectfully, employees can avoid misunderstandings that often lead to conflict. For instance, when a team member does not agree with a proposed strategy, using assertive communication to express their viewpoint can help the team consider alternative solutions without causing personal offense.

Moreover, assertiveness aids in setting professional boundaries. It empowers individuals to say no when necessary, which is vital for managing workload and preventing burnout. For example, an employee might use assertive communication to decline additional responsibilities that exceed their capacity, explaining their current commitments and suggesting an alternative timeline or delegation strategy.

Assertiveness also enhances leadership qualities. Leaders who communicate assertively are perceived as confident and trustworthy. They are better equipped to motivate their teams, provide clear instructions, and handle criticism constructively. An assertive leader who provides feedback on an employee's performance issue would do so by focusing on specific behaviors rather than personal attributes, thereby facilitating growth and development rather than causing resentment.

Incorporating assertiveness into workplace training programs can further enhance these skills among employees. Role-playing exercises that simulate challenging conversations can be particularly effective. These activities allow employees to practice responding to difficult situations in real-time, which builds confidence and helps them apply these skills during actual interactions.

In conclusion, cultivating assertiveness in workplace interactions not only improves individual performance but also contributes to a more harmonious organizational culture. By encouraging open dialogue and respectful communication practices, companies can foster environments where innovation thrives and conflicts are resolved constructively.

7.3 Navigating Social Situations with Confidence

Mastering assertive communication in social settings is pivotal for navigating various interactions with poise and assurance. This skill not only enhances personal relationships but also bolsters one's self-esteem by enabling clear and respectful expression of thoughts and feelings without overstepping others' boundaries.

Assertiveness in social scenarios involves more than just speaking up; it encompasses the ability to listen actively, respond appropriately, and maintain composure even in challenging situations. For instance, at a networking event, an assertive individual can introduce themselves confidently, engage in meaningful conversations without dominating them, and respectfully disagree when opinions diverge.

Effective assertive communication also includes non-verbal cues such as maintaining eye contact, using open body language, and modulating one's tone to match the conversation's context. These elements contribute significantly to how messages are perceived and received by others. A person who masters both verbal and non-verbal aspects of assertive communication is often seen as charismatic and approachable—qualities that are invaluable in any social circle.

Moreover, being assertive helps individuals set healthy personal boundaries. Clearly communicating one's limits in a friendly yet firm manner can prevent misunderstandings and reduce the likelihood of feeling overwhelmed or taken advantage of in social settings. For example, someone might decline an invitation due to prior commitments by expressing regret and suggesting an alternative time for meeting, thus maintaining the relationship while honoring their own schedule.

To cultivate this skill, individuals can practice through role-playing exercises with friends or mentors that simulate challenging social interactions. Feedback from these sessions can be incredibly beneficial for improving one's approach before applying it in real-world contexts. Additionally, observing how respected figures handle social situations can provide practical insights into effective strategies for assertive communication.

In conclusion, navigating social situations with confidence through assertive communication not only strengthens interpersonal relationships but also builds a foundation for personal growth and success across various life domains. By consistently practicing these skills, individuals can enhance their ability to interact authentically and effectively within any social framework.

8 Progressive Skill Building

8.1 Incremental Learning Approach to Skill Enhancement

The incremental learning approach is a strategic method that emphasizes gradual skill enhancement through small, manageable steps rather than attempting large leaps in capability all at once. This technique aligns closely with cognitive behavioral principles and neuroscience findings that suggest the brain adapts more effectively to consistent, slight changes over time.

At the core of this approach is the concept of building a "learning scaffold" where each new piece of knowledge or skill is carefully added to the existing framework of understanding. This method not only solidifies previous learning but also prepares the individual for more complex challenges ahead. It mirrors the natural learning process, akin to how one first learns to crawl, then walk, and finally run.

Practical application in daily life begins with setting clear, achievable goals. For instance, if someone wishes to become more assertive in workplace meetings, they might start by simply voicing their opinion once every session before gradually increasing their involvement. This could be further enhanced by reflective practices such as journaling or peer feedback, which help reinforce what was learned and identify areas for improvement.

Another vital component of the incremental learning approach is regular review and adjustment. As individuals progress, they should reassess their goals and learning strategies to ensure they remain aligned with their evolving skills and aspirations. This adaptive strategy not only maintains relevance but also keeps motivation high as learners see tangible progress.

The effectiveness of this approach can be significantly amplified by incorporating modern tools such as digital apps that track progress or provide virtual scenarios for practice. These technologies can offer immediate feedback and data-driven insights that are crucial for fine-tuning skills incrementally.

In conclusion, the incremental learning approach offers a practical pathway to skill enhancement that is deeply rooted in psychological research and educational theory. By embracing this method, individuals can transform daunting challenges into series of achievable victories, leading to sustained personal growth and improved self-efficacy.

8.2 Role-Playing Scenarios to Practice Responses

Role-playing scenarios are an essential tool in the incremental learning approach, particularly effective for practicing interpersonal skills and responses in a controlled, risk-free environment. This method allows individuals to experiment with various strategies and receive feedback in real-time, which is crucial for refining skills and building confidence.

One of the primary benefits of role-playing is its ability to simulate challenging interactions or situations that one might face in the workplace or daily life. For example, a person aiming to enhance their conflict resolution skills can engage in a scenario where they must address and settle a dispute between colleagues. This practice not only helps them apply theoretical knowledge but also aids in managing emotions and reactions under pressure.

Furthermore, role-playing adapts well to both individual and group training sessions. In individual settings, a coach or mentor can assume various roles, providing the learner with different perspectives and challenges. This setup is beneficial for personalized feedback and targeted skill development. In group settings, participants can rotate roles among themselves, which fosters empathy by understanding different viewpoints and enhances communication skills through direct peer interaction.

To maximize the effectiveness of role-playing exercises, it is important to follow a structured process that includes preparation, action, observation, and reflection. Initially, participants should be given a clear context and objectives for the scenario. During the role-play, observers (either coaches or peers) should note key moments where the participant's responses were effective or could be improved. After the exercise, a detailed debriefing session allows for discussion of what was learned during the role-play. This reflection phase is critical as it helps consolidate learning by connecting actions with outcomes.

Incorporating technology can further enhance these scenarios through virtual reality (VR) environments that create more immersive experiences without real-world consequences. VR enables complex interpersonal interactions to be simulated with greater emotional intensity compared to traditional role-plays.

In conclusion, role-playing scenarios serve as a dynamic training tool within the incremental learning framework that significantly improves practical response strategies while enhancing emotional intelligence and situational awareness.

8.3 Feedback Mechanisms for Continuous Improvement

Feedback mechanisms are integral to the process of continuous improvement in skill development, serving as a bridge between theoretical learning and practical application. These mechanisms allow individuals to understand their performance in real-world scenarios and refine their skills accordingly. Effective feedback systems are characterized by their specificity, timeliness, and relevance, which help learners make precise adjustments to their behavior or strategies.

One effective approach is the use of digital platforms that provide immediate feedback during training exercises. For instance, software tools can simulate customer service situations where learners respond to virtual customers, and the system provides instant feedback based on the learner's choices. This technology not only points out what was done well but also highlights areas for improvement and suggests methods to handle similar situations better in the future.

Another critical aspect of feedback mechanisms is peer review sessions following role-playing exercises or group tasks. Here, participants engage in constructive dialogue about each other's performance. This peer-to-peer interaction encourages a deeper understanding of diverse perspectives and promotes a supportive learning environment where individuals feel valued and motivated to improve.

Moreover, incorporating structured reflection sessions after each exercise enhances the learning process significantly. During these sessions, facilitators guide learners through a detailed analysis of their actions and the outcomes thereof. Learners discuss what they intended versus what actually happened, dissecting discrepancies and planning future modifications in behavior or strategy. This reflective practice not only consolidates learning but also empowers individuals by making them active participants in their own development journey.

To further enrich this feedback loop, some organizations implement 360-degree feedback systems where employees receive anonymous reviews from peers, subordinates, and supervisors. Such comprehensive input provides a holistic view of an individual's skills and behaviors across various interactions within the organization. It helps pinpoint specific areas needing attention while affirmatively acknowledging strengths.

In conclusion, robust feedback mechanisms are crucial for fostering an environment of continuous improvement within any learning framework. By systematically integrating these tools into training programs—whether through technology-assisted simulations, peer reviews, reflective practices, or comprehensive 360-degree evaluations—organizations can significantly enhance individual competencies that are critical for personal growth and organizational success.

9 Overcoming Setbacks

9.1 Identifying Triggers and Learning from Failures

Understanding the triggers that lead to setbacks and learning from failures are crucial steps in personal development and building resilience. This section delves into the mechanisms of identifying what prompts setbacks and how to extract valuable lessons from failures, ultimately turning them into stepping stones for success.

Identifying triggers involves a deep dive into one's reactions to various situations. Triggers can be emotional, situational, or relational. Emotional triggers might include feelings of inadequacy or anxiety when faced with specific tasks or social settings. Situational triggers could be related to particular environments like high-pressure meetings or public speaking events. Relational triggers often involve interactions with certain individuals who might challenge our self-esteem or decision-making capabilities.

To effectively identify these triggers, individuals are encouraged to maintain a reflective journal where they can document specific instances that led to feelings of setback or failure. This practice not only aids in recognizing patterns but also helps in managing emotional responses more constructively. For instance, if one notices that criticism from a superior consistently leads to a drop in productivity, they can prepare by seeking feedback regularly in smaller doses to lessen the impact when it comes unexpectedly.

Learning from failures is equally important as identifying triggers. It requires an open-minded approach where failures are not seen as embarrassments but as rich sources of insight. Analyzing what went wrong in any given situation provides practical clues on what needs improvement. Whether it's a failed project at work or a personal goal that wasn't met, dissecting the sequence of actions leading up to the failure can reveal missteps and areas for enhancement.

Moreover, discussing these experiences with mentors or peers can provide external perspectives and solutions that might not be apparent from a singular viewpoint. Such discussions can also foster a culture of transparency and continuous improvement both personally and professionally.

In conclusion, by identifying triggers and learning from failures, individuals equip themselves with knowledge about their behavioral patterns and practical strategies for overcoming future challenges. This proactive approach not only enhances personal growth but also contributes significantly to building enduring self-confidence and resilience.

9.2 Maintaining Motivation During Challenges

Maintaining motivation in the face of challenges is essential for personal and professional growth. This section explores strategies to sustain drive and enthusiasm during difficult periods, ensuring continuous progress towards goals despite setbacks.

One effective method to maintain motivation is setting clear, achievable goals. Breaking larger objectives into smaller, manageable tasks can help maintain a sense of accomplishment and momentum. For instance, if the goal is to write a book, setting daily word count targets can provide immediate satisfaction and encourage steady progress.

Another crucial strategy is maintaining a positive mindset. Challenges often bring frustration and negativity, which can diminish motivation. Cultivating an optimistic outlook involves reframing obstacles as opportunities to learn and grow rather than insurmountable problems. Techniques such as mindfulness meditation or positive affirmations can aid in developing this mindset.

Support systems play a pivotal role in sustaining motivation during tough times. Surrounding oneself with encouraging friends, family members, or colleagues can provide emotional support and practical advice when facing difficulties. Additionally, joining groups or communities with similar goals can offer motivation through shared experiences and collective encouragement.

Visual reminders of one's goals can also serve as powerful motivators. Creating vision boards or setting up notifications with inspiring quotes can reinforce commitment to the end goal and boost morale when enthusiasm wanes.

Rewarding oneself for small victories is another effective motivational tool. Establishing rewards for each milestone achieved not only creates pleasure but also reinforces the behavior needed to succeed. These rewards could range from taking a day off to enjoy a favorite activity to smaller treats like enjoying a special meal.

In conclusion, maintaining motivation amidst challenges requires a multifaceted approach that includes setting achievable goals, fostering a positive mindset, leveraging support systems, using visual reminders, and rewarding oneself for progress made. By implementing these strategies consistently, individuals can ensure they remain driven and focused on their path to success even during difficult times.

9.3 Adaptive Strategies for Resilience

Building resilience in the face of adversity is crucial for sustained success and well-being. This section delves into adaptive strategies that individuals can employ to enhance their resilience, enabling them to bounce back from setbacks more effectively and maintain progress towards their goals.

One foundational strategy is the development of a flexible mindset. Unlike a fixed mindset, which sees challenges as permanent and insurmountable, a flexible mindset embraces challenges as opportunities for growth and learning. This shift in perspective allows individuals to adapt more readily to changing circumstances and view setbacks as temporary hurdles rather than definitive failures.

Another vital component of resilience is emotional regulation. Managing one's emotions in response to stress or disappointment is essential for maintaining mental health and focus. Techniques such as deep breathing exercises, progressive muscle relaxation, or engaging in regular physical activity can help mitigate the intensity of negative emotions, fostering a calmer, more composed approach to problem-solving.

Proactive problem-solving is also integral to resilience. Instead of avoiding issues, resilient individuals confront challenges head-on by developing actionable plans. This might involve seeking advice from mentors, brainstorming potential solutions, or breaking down large problems into smaller, more manageable parts. By actively engaging with difficulties, individuals not only find practical solutions but also build confidence in their ability to handle future obstacles.

Social support networks are equally important for resilience. Having close connections with friends, family, or colleagues provides not just emotional comfort but also practical assistance during tough times. These relationships can offer different perspectives on a problem, suggest solutions previously unconsidered, or simply provide encouragement that boosts morale and motivation.

In conclusion, adaptive strategies such as developing a flexible mindset, regulating emotions effectively, engaging in proactive problem-solving, leveraging social support networks, and committing to continuous learning are essential for fostering resilience. Implementing these strategies helps individuals navigate through challenges more successfully while supporting personal growth and achievement.

Lastly, continuous learning and self-improvement play a critical role in building resilience. By consistently acquiring new skills and knowledge, individuals prepare themselves better for unexpected changes and are less likely to be overwhelmed by them. Whether through formal education, self-study, or professional development activities, enhancing one's skill set can significantly contribute to a resilient outlook.

Long-Term Success in Confidence Maintenance

10.1 Incorporating Mindfulness into Daily Routine

Mindfulness, a practice rooted in ancient tradition, has gained modern relevance as a foundational tool in enhancing self-esteem and assertiveness. By integrating mindfulness into daily routines, individuals can cultivate a heightened awareness of their thoughts and emotions, leading to more deliberate and confident interactions. This section explores practical ways to embed mindfulness practices into everyday life, thereby supporting long-term confidence maintenance.

The first step in incorporating mindfulness is to establish a consistent daily practice that acts as an anchor. Simple activities such as mindful breathing or focused attention on sensory experiences can be integrated seamlessly into morning routines. For instance, spending five minutes each morning practicing deep breathing exercises can set a calm and centered tone for the day. This not only reduces stress but also empowers individuals to handle challenging situations with greater poise and assurance.

Another effective strategy is the use of mindful walking during commutes or breaks. Instead of rushing from point A to B, one could focus on the sensation of walking, noticing the rhythm of steps or the feel of the ground underfoot. This practice transforms mundane activities into opportunities for mindfulness, encouraging a present-centered mindset throughout the day.

Beyond individual practices, creating mindful spaces at home or work can also support this endeavor. Designating specific areas that are free from distractions where one can meditate or engage in quiet reflection encourages regular practice. Additionally, technology offers various tools such as apps that guide users through mindfulness exercises tailored for different times of the day or specific challenges like anxiety reduction.

Engage in short mindfulness exercises before important meetings or presentations to foster calmness and clarity.

Incorporate mindful eating during meals by paying close attention to the flavors, textures, and sensations involved, which enhances enjoyment and promotes better digestion.

End each day with a brief reflection on moments where mindfulness was successfully applied and identify areas for improvement.

In conclusion, integrating mindfulness into daily routines does not require drastic changes; rather it involves small but meaningful adjustments that promote awareness and presence. Over time, these practices enhance one's ability to remain composed under pressure and communicate assertively—key components of sustained confidence and success.

10.2 Continuous Learning and Adaptation

Continuous learning and adaptation are essential for maintaining and enhancing confidence over the long term. This section delves into how embracing a mindset geared towards ongoing education and flexibility can significantly bolster self-assurance in various aspects of life, from professional endeavors to personal relationships.

The importance of continuous learning in confidence building cannot be overstated. In a rapidly changing world, acquiring new skills and knowledge not only makes an individual more competent but also more confident in their ability to handle future challenges. This process involves actively seeking out educational opportunities, whether formal or informal, such as online courses, workshops, or books that cover new theories and practical applications within one's field or interests.

Adaptation plays a crucial role alongside learning. It refers to the ability to adjust one's behavior and thoughts in response to new situations or information. This flexibility can be particularly empowering in unfamiliar or challenging circumstances. For instance, when faced with a career change or a difficult life event, being able to adapt effectively can maintain one's self-esteem and mitigate feelings of uncertainty or stress.

Engage regularly in training sessions that not only focus on skill enhancement but also on developing adaptive thinking and problem-solving abilities.

Create personal learning projects that challenge existing knowledge bases and push boundaries, thus fostering both intellectual growth and self-confidence.

Practice reflective habits by journaling or through discussions with mentors to evaluate learning experiences and adapt strategies accordingly.

To integrate continuous learning and adaptation into daily life effectively, it is beneficial to develop habits that encourage curiosity and open-mindedness. Setting aside time each week for reflection on what has been learned and how it applies to personal growth or career advancement can make this process part of a routine rather than an occasional activity.

In conclusion, continuous learning coupled with the ability to adapt are dynamic tools for sustaining confidence. They equip individuals not only with necessary skills but also with the mental agility required to thrive in diverse environments, thereby reinforcing a robust sense of self-worth over time.

10.3 Building a Support Network

Building a robust support network is crucial for long-term confidence maintenance. This network, comprising friends, family, colleagues, and mentors, provides emotional backing, practical advice, and diverse perspectives that can significantly enhance one's ability to navigate challenges and opportunities with greater assurance.

The foundation of a strong support network starts with identifying individuals who positively influence your personal and professional growth. These are people who encourage you to step out of your comfort zone while providing a safety net of guidance and support. Cultivating these relationships involves regular communication, mutual respect, and an understanding of shared as well as individual goals.

Professional networks are equally important in building confidence. They not only offer insights into industry trends and skills necessary for career advancement but also provide opportunities for collaboration that might not be available within an immediate work environment. Engaging in professional associations or online communities related to your field can expand your network beyond geographical limitations.

Mentorship plays a pivotal role in confidence building through support networks. A mentor can offer not just guidance based on their own experiences but also serve as a sounding board for ideas and frustrations. Whether formal or informal, these mentoring relationships foster an environment where learning from failures is encouraged, thereby boosting resilience and self-confidence.

To effectively leverage your support network, it's essential to be proactive in your interactions. This could mean setting up regular check-ins with mentors, participating actively in community events, or simply sharing updates with those in your network to keep the lines of communication open.

In conclusion, a well-rounded support network is invaluable for maintaining confidence over the long term. It provides not only emotional encouragement but also practical help and professional guidance necessary to navigate the complexities of both personal development and career progression.

Special Considerations in the Journey to Confid

11.1 Addressing Anxiety and Depression

In the quest for confidence, addressing underlying mental health challenges such as anxiety and depression is crucial. These conditions can severely impact one's self-esteem and hinder the development of assertive communication skills. Understanding and managing these issues are therefore fundamental steps in fostering a resilient sense of self-worth.

Anxiety and depression often manifest through persistent negative thoughts and doubts that can overshadow an individual's perceptions of their abilities and worth. Cognitive Behavioral Therapy (CBT), a key focus in "Confidence Unleashed," offers strategies to counteract these distortions. CBT techniques such as cognitive restructuring involve identifying and challenging harmful thought patterns, enabling individuals to develop more balanced and positive thinking.

Moreover, mindfulness practices are highlighted as effective tools for managing symptoms of both anxiety and depression. Mindfulness helps individuals anchor themselves in the present moment, reducing the prevalence of ruminative thoughts that often accompany these conditions. By incorporating mindfulness into daily routines, readers can enhance their mental clarity and emotional stability, creating a stronger foundation for confidence.

The journey towards overcoming anxiety and depression is deeply personal yet universally relevant in building confidence. "Confidence Unleashed" not only equips its readers with theoretical knowledge but also encourages practical application through exercises designed to apply CBT principles in everyday situations. This dual approach ensures that individuals do not merely understand the concepts intellectually but also integrate them into their lives, leading to lasting changes in how they view themselves and interact with others.

Engaging in regular physical activity which has been shown to reduce symptoms of both anxiety and depression by releasing endorphins that promote a sense of well-being.

Establishing a consistent sleep schedule to improve mood regulation and cognitive function, making it easier to engage with assertive communication practices.

Nurturing social connections which provide emotional support and reinforce feelings of self-worth through positive interactions.

In conclusion, effectively addressing anxiety and depression is integral to unlocking one's potential for developing true confidence. Through targeted strategies like CBT, mindfulness, physical wellness, consistent sleep patterns, and strong social networks, individuals can overcome these barriers. This holistic approach empowers readers to reclaim control over their mental health and pave the way for a more assertive, confident self.

11.2 Tailoring Approaches for Different Personality Types

Understanding that each individual's path to confidence is influenced by their unique personality type is crucial in crafting effective personal development strategies. Personality types, as defined by various psychological frameworks, significantly affect how people perceive themselves and interact with the world. This section explores how tailored approaches can enhance the journey to confidence for different personality types.

For instance, introverted individuals often require different strategies compared to their extroverted counterparts. Introverts might find confidence in environments that allow for deep thinking and less social interaction, whereas extroverts may thrive in more dynamic and interactive settings. Recognizing these needs is key to providing support that resonates with an individual's intrinsic tendencies.

Similarly, those with a detail-oriented nature, often categorized under analytical personality types, might benefit from structured and well-defined steps towards building confidence. These individuals appreciate clarity and are likely to engage more effectively with programs that offer concrete data and systematic progress tracking.

On the other hand, intuitive personalities might prefer a more holistic approach. They tend to look at the bigger picture and could find value in methods that emphasize understanding underlying emotions and developing interpersonal skills through varied experiences rather than rigid structures.

The assertive versus sensitive dichotomy also plays a significant role in tailoring confidence-building strategies. Assertive individuals may excel in scenarios where they can lead and influence others, gaining confidence from direct achievements and leadership roles. Sensitive personalities might develop confidence through validation of their feelings and thoughts, benefiting from environments where empathy and understanding are prioritized.

To effectively address these diverse needs, it is essential for coaches or self-help programs like "Confidence Unleashed" to incorporate a range of tools and techniques suitable for different personality spectrums. Activities such as role-playing can help extroverts and assertives engage actively, while journaling or private reflection sessions may be more beneficial for introverts or sensitive types.

In conclusion, recognizing the diversity in personality types allows for a more personalized approach in helping individuals build confidence. By adapting strategies to meet specific psychological profiles, one can foster a deeper sense of self-awareness and empowerment among those seeking to enhance their self-esteem.

11.3 Cultural Influences on Assertiveness

Assertiveness, a key component in building confidence, is significantly shaped by cultural backgrounds. Different cultures have varied expectations and norms that influence how individuals express themselves and assert their needs. This section explores how these cultural nuances impact the development of assertive behaviors and the strategies that can be employed to navigate them effectively.

In collectivist societies, such as those in many Asian countries, the emphasis is often on community and harmony rather than individual expression. Assertiveness may be perceived negatively, associated with selfishness or disruption of peace. In these environments, indirect communication styles are prevalent, where subtlety and implication play crucial roles in conveying messages. Understanding these dynamics is essential for individuals from such backgrounds to develop a form of assertiveness that respects cultural norms while effectively expressing personal needs.

Conversely, in individualistic cultures like the United States or Western Europe, direct communication and assertiveness are generally valued and encouraged. Here, assertiveness is often seen as a sign of leadership and self-confidence. Individuals from these cultures may find it easier to express their opinions openly and advocate for themselves without fearing social repercussions.

The challenge arises when people from collectivist backgrounds interact in predominantly individualistic settings or vice versa. For instance, a Japanese professional working in an American company might struggle with being direct enough to meet the expectations of their role. Similarly, an American working in Japan might find their usual directness perceived as rude or disrespectful.

To bridge these cultural gaps, it's important for global businesses and multicultural teams to foster environments where diverse communication styles are understood and respected. Training programs that focus on intercultural communication can equip individuals with the tools to adjust their level of assertiveness according to the cultural context they are operating within.

Moreover, personal development coaches working with clients from various cultural backgrounds should tailor their approaches based on an understanding of these cultural influences on assertiveness. By doing so, they can help clients navigate both their personal and professional lives more effectively, ensuring that they remain true to themselves while being culturally sensitive.

In conclusion, recognizing the profound impact of cultural influences on assertive behavior is crucial for anyone looking to build confidence across diverse environments. By adapting strategies that consider these differences, individuals can enhance their interpersonal effectiveness and achieve greater success in global settings.

12 Conclusion and Future Directions

12.1 Summarizing Key Takeaways

In the realm of personal development, "Confidence Unleashed: How to Build Self-Esteem and Assertiveness" serves as a crucial resource for individuals seeking to navigate the complexities of self-perception and interaction in a fast-paced world. This section encapsulates the core insights derived from the book, emphasizing practical strategies that foster self-assurance and effective communication.

The journey begins with an exploration of the psychological underpinnings of self-esteem and assertiveness. By integrating findings from cognitive behavioral therapy (CBT), social psychology, and neuroscience, the book provides a robust framework for understanding the origins and impacts of self-doubt. Readers are guided through a process of identifying personal patterns of negative thinking that frequently sabotage confidence. This foundational knowledge is vital as it sets the stage for transformative change.

Transitioning from theory to practice, "Confidence Unleashed" introduces a series of actionable steps designed to be implemented immediately. These include diverse exercises that encourage self-reflection and gradual engagement with assertive communication techniques. For instance, readers might begin with simple affirmations to bolster their sense of self-worth before progressing to more complex interpersonal scenarios where these skills are put to test. Such structured progression ensures not only comprehension but also practical competence in navigating social interactions confidently.

The final chapters focus on sustainability—maintaining and growing one's newfound confidence. Here, resilience becomes a key theme; readers learn strategies for dealing with setbacks effectively and viewing challenges as opportunities for growth. Emphasis is placed on continuous practice and mindfulness, reinforcing the idea that confidence building is an ongoing journey rather than a finite goal.

Overall, "Confidence Unleashed" equips its readers not just with theoretical knowledge but with real-world tools that promise significant improvements in how they view themselves and interact with others. It stands out as an empowering guide that transforms theoretical concepts into actionable steps that lead to tangible enhancements in personal and professional realms.

12.2 Encouraging Lifelong Practice

The pursuit of self-confidence and assertiveness is not a destination but a continuous journey. Encouraging lifelong practice in these areas is crucial for sustained personal growth and effectiveness in interpersonal interactions. This section delves into strategies that help maintain and enhance the gains achieved through initial training, as outlined in "Confidence Unleashed."

Firstly, establishing a routine of regular self-reflection is vital. Individuals are encouraged to set aside time each week to reflect on their progress and challenges in building confidence and practicing assertiveness. This could involve journaling or meditation sessions where one can introspect on recent interactions and personal feelings, assessing areas for improvement.

Secondly, the role of community support cannot be overstated. Engaging with groups or forums where individuals share similar goals can provide motivation and insight, which are essential for long-term adherence to any personal development plan. Whether it's through online platforms or local meetups, connecting with others offers both accountability and encouragement.

Another significant aspect involves ongoing education. The landscape of self-improvement continuously evolves with new research and methodologies emerging regularly. Participants should be encouraged to stay updated by attending workshops, reading relevant books, or enrolling in courses that focus on advanced communication skills, emotional intelligence, and other related topics.

Moreover, setting incremental goals plays a critical role in lifelong practice. Instead of overwhelming oneself with large objectives, breaking them down into smaller, manageable tasks can lead to consistent progress. Celebrating small victories also boosts morale and reinforces the value of persistent effort.

Lastly, adapting practices to suit changing life circumstances is essential for maintaining relevance and effectiveness of the techniques learned. As individuals grow professionally and personally, their needs and environments change; thus, the application of confidence-building strategies must also evolve.

In conclusion, encouraging lifelong practice in developing confidence and assertiveness requires a multifaceted approach involving regular self-assessment, community involvement, continued learning, goal setting, and adaptability. By integrating these elements into daily life, individuals can ensure that they not only achieve but also sustain the high levels of self-esteem necessary for successful personal and professional interactions.

12.3 Resources for Further Exploration

In the journey of fostering self-confidence and assertiveness, continuous learning plays a pivotal role. This section outlines various resources that individuals can utilize to further their understanding and skills in these areas, ensuring sustained growth beyond initial training.

Firstly, books and literature offer a wealth of knowledge. Titles such as "Daring Greatly" by Brené Brown or "The Confidence Code" by Katty Kay and Claire Shipman provide insights into the psychological underpinnings of confidence and practical advice for everyday application. These readings serve not only as guides but also as sources of inspiration to continue the practice of self-reflection and assertiveness.

Secondly, online courses present an accessible avenue for structured learning. Platforms like Coursera or Udemy feature courses on topics ranging from emotional intelligence to effective communication skills. These courses are often led by industry experts and provide flexibility in learning pace, making it easier for individuals to integrate new knowledge into their busy schedules.

Additionally, podcasts have emerged as a popular medium for on-the-go learning. Podcasts such as "The Art of Charm" or "The School of Greatness" offer episodes that delve into personal development themes with guest speakers who share real-world experiences and actionable tips.

Engaging with professional groups or clubs such as Toastmasters can also be incredibly beneficial. Such communities not only provide a platform to practice learned skills but also offer feedback from peers who are similarly committed to personal growth in confidence and assertiveness.

Lastly, attending workshops and seminars offers direct interaction with thought leaders and coaches who specialize in personal development. These live events often include exercises that help solidify the concepts covered, providing participants with hands-on experience in applying new strategies within group settings.

To conclude, expanding one's resource pool is crucial for ongoing advancement in building self-confidence and assertiveness. By leveraging books, online courses, podcasts, community groups, and live workshops, individuals can maintain momentum in their developmental journey while adapting to new challenges and opportunities that arise throughout their lives.

"Confidence Unleashed: How to Build Self-Esteem and Assertiveness" serves as a comprehensive guide aimed at empowering individuals who struggle with self-doubt and a lack of assertiveness. Addressing the widespread issue of low self-esteem, which impacts an estimated 85% of the global population, this book provides practical strategies rooted in cognitive behavioral therapy (CBT), social psychology, and neuroscience. It explores the psychological underpinnings of why people experience low confidence and how they can transform their thought patterns and behaviors.

The book is structured to first help readers recognize and address their own negative thoughts and behaviors that sabotage confidence. It offers a variety of strategies to overcome these initial barriers. Progressing from theory to practice, the subsequent sections provide actionable steps that include exercises for self-reflection and applying assertive communication techniques in daily interactions. These exercises range from simple affirmations to complex real-world scenarios, ensuring that readers can gradually build on their new skills.

Finally, "Confidence Unleashed" concludes with guidance on maintaining confidence over time. This section emphasizes resilience, teaching readers how to handle setbacks effectively and view challenges as opportunities for growth. Through continuous practice and mindfulness, the book aims to equip readers not only with theoretical knowledge but also with practical tools that foster long-term success in personal empowerment.

Overall, this transformative guide promises not just insights but tangible changes in both personal and professional realms, helping individuals become more confident and assertive through well-founded methods.

www.ingramcontent.com/pod-product-compliance
Lightning Source LLC
Chambersburg PA
CBHW072000210526
45479CB00003B/1009